piano • vocal • guitar

A N T H O L O G Y

T0044918

This publication is not for sale in
the E.C. and/or Australia
or New Zealand.

ISBN 0-7935-6806-4

CONTENTS

WAR

There was war on the streets and abroad. In South Central L.A., Compton, Long Beach–on the same streets that twenty years later would trigger gangsta rap–there was a group of friends who grew up in the same neighborhood, shared the same experiences, and showed a way other than war. They spoke of racism and hunger, of gangs and turf wars and low riders, and in the music they made reflected the hope for a spirit of brotherhood.

WAR was a crossover phenomenon that finally and forever fused rock, jazz, funk, Latin, and R&B. Transcending cultural barriers with a multi-ethnic lineup, WAR was a musical melting pot and an enduring influence.

But today there is still war on the street. And today WAR is back.

"The world is *still* a ghetto," says WAR's founding keyboardist and vocalist Lonnie Jordan, echoing the title of their best-selling classic album and song. "We haven't grown; we're the same. People get together for fifteen minutes, but then they're back to their cubbyholes and forget togetherness. Racism hasn't changed. 'Why Can't We Be Friends?' and 'Can't we all just get along?' sound alike to me. There will always be a reason to play 'Don't Let No One Get You Down', 'Me and Baby Brother,' or 'Why Can't We Be Friends?'"

LONNIE JORDAN

On **Peace Sign** (Avenue Records #71706), the band's eighteenth major-label album, WAR proves to be as relevant as ever, and as funky.

"How long did it take us to make this album?" Jordan asks. "Thirteen years: twelve growing and evolving, and one in the studio."

In the early eighties, disco and its formulaic beats-per-minute put a damper on WAR's phenomenal successs—after selling more than 23 million records, including a triple-platinum -selling album (**The World Is a Ghetto**), two double-platinum-selling albums (**Greatest Hits** and **Why Can't We Be Friends?**), four platinum-selling-albums (**Deliver the Word**, **WAR Live**, **All Day Music**, and **Platinum Jazz**), three gold-selling albums (**Eric Burdon Declares WAR**, **Galaxy**, **The Music Band**, plus their newest soon-to-be platinum addition, **The Best of WAR...and More**), and six

HOWARD SCOTT

gold singles.

Appropriately, it was a new street music—rap and hip-hop—that helped bring WAR back. WAR's grooves were being sampled by practitioners of the new art form, and songs such as "Slippin' into Darkness," "The Cisco Kid," and "Low Rider" were being discovered by a new audience. The 1992 Rap Declares WAR album collection of these rap-and-WAR tracks marked the band's reintroduction. Peace Sign marks its rebirth.

ERIC BURDON

From the first notes of the funky "Peace Sign," you know this is WAR. Whether the loco "Wild Rodriguez" or the pop "What If" with its positive message of "What if everybody gave up their guns and dope/There'd be a lot more joy and hope"; whether "East L.A.," its sixties pop marrying a salsa beat and friend Jose Feliciano adding vocals in Spanish; or the soulful protest of "Homeless Hero", or silky smooth "U B O K" and "The

Smuggler"; WAR's extended songs with jazzy horn breaks and social consciousness are both gritty and lyrical, infectious and easy. WAR reaches into the soul and moves people.

"When you come back to reality, you pull down WAR because WAR is reality," says drummer Ronnie Hammon. Lonnie Jordan agrees: "We have a lot of second generation fans and they're seeing the same things their parents saw. They're hearing the same messages."

It's no surprise that recent movies such as **Dazed & Confused**, **Mi Vida Loca**, **Colors**, and TNT's **The Cisco Kid** have featured vintage music by WAR. But it's the present and future that interest the band members.

B.B. DICKERSON

Says Jordan of Peace Sign: "This is the most musically satisfying project we've ever done, because of the blood, sweat, and tears that went into it and because its message is very clear and strong. Once again, we're able to deliver the word. This is street music, all kinds of streets—Wilshire, Compton, Sunset, or in the alley. It's the feeling of the people, the beat. We never left the streets."

ERIC BURDON & WAR

When the gold albums stopped coming in the early eighties, they took to the streets again, playing every waterhole from west to east and across Europe and Japan. Though it changed its stage clothes, WAR never changed its music for the sake of economics. Hammon says, "We don't know how to become dishonest musicians." So they played on.

What WAR did was to stay true to its music and itself. Says Jordan, "We were the same people before we made it, when we made it, and when we were coming down. Success becomes a burden only when you try to be what you're not. That'll destroy you."

WAR found that its music wasn't nostalgia, but instead had been way ahead of the times—ahead of the Latin influence in pop, ahead of the World Beat, ahead of crossover R&B. The times simply had to catch up with them. "We're like Levis," says Hammon, "and there's nothing nostalgic about Levis." In fact," adds Scott, "they're not really good and funky until they've been worn awhile." When Brown found that his own copies of their albums were missing because his son had taken them to parties—even though some of the records were older than his son—he knew that WAR still had something to say.

What WAR had to say rested in who they were as people. "We were a big old gumbo, a Creole mixture," says Brown. Growing up, Long Beach was a mixture of whites, blacks browns, reds, and yellows. "We thought that was normal," he says. And it showed in their music.

LEE OSKAR

In the seven years before the band was transformed into WAR, it had a following in R&B clubs backing the likes of Marvin Gaye and Little Willie John. At the same time, it was breaking down the walls when it became the first local black group booked on the Sunset Strip, playing rock clubs like the legendary Cinnamon Cinder on bills with white teenagers such as the Ventures.

"We never thought we'd hit, because we were too different," recalls

Jordan. "People wanted us to be like the Chambers Brothers or Sly and the Family Stone. But we just let it flow and played." One show, at the Fillmore West, consisted of just one song that moved from blues to psychedelic to rock to R&B. "We performed without the format and without the fear."

CHARLES MILLER

WAR's strength is in its spontaneity, its ability to improvise. "Why Can't We Be Friends?" was composed backstage while waiting to go on. A ruckus had broken out and the band left the dressing room to check what was happening. When they returned, they just started singing. From that jam, a classic unforgettable song was born. None other than Jimi Hendrix was amazed at WAR's ability to create songs jamming till four in the morning. And it continues: recently, at a concert in San Francisco, the band was playing and Jordan heard something he liked and suddenly a jam started and WAR was, well, WAR again.

Despite its name, WAR has been a positive force in music. "At first it was taken negarively," explains Hammon, "that war is conflict. But war starts with inner conflict, your mind can be the genesis of war. If you can conquer it there, then you will have peace." Says Jordan, "It was us making war against war." WAR did not preach, but it asked the right question: Why?

It still does. In "Homeless Hero," on Peace Sign, WAR takes a character back from Vietnam, affected by drugs and alcohol, thrown on the streets with no skills but how to kill, and asks why? "When each person deals with the answer in his soul," stated Howard Scott, "Then the world will be a better place."

Brotherhood is not merely a buzzword for these musicians. Togetherness is what WAR has stood for, musically and as a group of people, for three decades. Says Lonnie Jordan, "We've been through puberty together, through first loves, first heartbreaks, first marriages, first sons and daug\hters, joyous moments of having our first hit together and moments of silence."

There is not another band in music history that can claim going from war to peace.

ERIC BURDON & WAR

WAR is:

Lonnie Jordan (keyboards, bass, vocals)

Ronnie Hammon (drums, vocals)

Rae Valentine (keyboards)

Kerry Campbell (saxophone)

Tetsuya "Tex" Nakamura (harmonica)

Richard Marquez (percussion)

JB Eckl (guitar)

FROM LEFT : LONNIE JORDAN; WAR PRODUCER JERRY GOLDSTEIN; EGYPTIAN PRESIDENT ANWAR SADAT'S YOUNGEST DAUGHTER; GAMAL SADAT'S FIANCEE DINA; ANWAR SADAT'S SON GAMAL; HOWARD SCOTT

WAR TODAY

ALL DAY MUSIC

Words and Music by SYLVESTER ALLEN, HAROLD R. BROWN,
MORRIS DICKERSON, LONNIE JORDAN, CHARLES W. MILLER,
LEE OSKAR, HOWARD SCOTT and JERRY GOLDSTEIN

Down at the beach or a par-ty in town_ Mak-ing love or just rid-ing a-round,

Let's have a pic - nic, go to the park,_ Roll-in' in the grass till long af-ter dark._

CINCO DE MAYO

Words and Music by SYLVESTER ALLEN, HAROLD R. BROWN,
JERRY GOLDSTEIN, LONNIE JORDAN, LEE OSKAR, HOWARD SCOTT,
RON HAMMON, PAT RIZZO and LUTHER RABB

Cin - co de May - o,

To Coda

Cin - co de May - o."

Cin-co de May - o,

Cin-co de May - o.

THE CISCO KID

Words and Music by SYLVESTER ALLEN, HAROLD R. BROWN,
MORRIS DICKERSON, LONNIE JORDAN,
CHARLES W. MILLER, LEE OSKAR and HOWARD SCOTT

Cis - co Kid was a friend_ of mine___

CITY, COUNTRY, CITY

Words and Music by SYLVESTER ALLEN, HAROLD R. BROWN,
MORRIS DICKERSON, LONNIE JORDAN,
CHARLES W. MILLER, LEE OSKAR and HOWARD SCOTT

DELIVER THE WORD

Words and Music by SYLVESTER ALLEN, HAROLD R. BROWN,
MORRIS DICKERSON, LONNIE JORDAN,
CHARLES W. MILLER, LEE OSKAR and HOWARD SCOTT

time, It's good for your mind. It makes you wan-na say

2.

chil-dren sing,__ full of joy,

Just like hav-ing a brand new, new,__ new toy.__ It makes you say

Repeat and fade

La la la la la la la la la,

DON'T LET NO ONE GET YOU DOWN

Words and Music by SYLVESTER ALLEN, HAROLD R. BROWN,
MORRIS DICKERSON, LONNIE JORDAN,
CHARLES W. MILLER, LEE OSKAR, HOWARD SCOTT and JERRY GOLDSTEIN

Ad lib. vocal above vamp
I'll keep you free, try
I'll bring you up, never down
You keep me happy all the time

GYPSY MAN

Words and Music by SYLVESTER ALLEN, HAROLD R. BROWN,
MORRIS DICKERSON, LONNIE JORDAN,
CHARLES W. MILLER, LEE OSKAR and HOWARD SCOTT

'Cause I'm a Gyp-sy Man.___ Yes, I'm a

Gyp-sy Man.___ Oh, I'm a Gyp-sy Man.___

Ooh ooh ooh___ ooh ooh ooh ooh ooh.___

Repeat and fade

Repeat and fade

GALAXY

Words and Music by SYLVESTER ALLEN, HAROLD R. BROWN,
MORRIS DICKERSON, LONNIE JORDAN, CHARLES W. MILLER,
LEE OSKAR, HOWARD SCOTT and JERRY GOLDSTEIN

Take me to your place in space. _ I'm
take you out to see the place, _ where the
Peo - ple mov - in' to and fro _ to a
Ninth dim - en - sion, sev - enth plane, _

sick and tired _ of the rat race. _ On a
man in the moon has a smil - in' face. You don't
sol - id band and a la - ser show. Su - per -
out here rais - ing sol - ar cane. The

L.A. SUNSHINE

Words and Music by SYLVESTER ALLEN, HAROLD R. BROWN,
MORRIS DICKERSON, LONNIE JORDAN, CHARLES W. MILLER,
LEE OSKAR, HOWARD SCOTT and JERRY GOLDSTEIN

Get on down, get on down, get on down.

Get on down, get on down, get on down in my

funk - y town, in my

funk - y town.

Repeat and Fade

LOW RIDER

Words and Music by SYLVESTER ALLEN, HAROLD R. BROWN,
MORRIS DICKERSON, JERRY GOLDSTEIN,
LEROY JORDAN, LEE OSKAR, CHARLES W. MILLER and HOWARD SCOTT

To Coda

Low rid – er drives a lit-tle slow – er, The
Low rid – er knows ev 'ry street, yeah!

low rid – er is a re-al go – er.
low rid – er is the one to meet, yeah! Low rid –

OUTLAW

Words and Music by SYLVESTER ALLEN, HAROLD R. BROWN,
JERRY GOLDSTEIN, LONNIE JORDAN, LEE OSKAR,
HOWARD SCOTT, RON HAMMON and LUTHER RABB

Moderate funky beat

The San Jo - se to the East L. A. I'm a
chopped - up Har - ley, pow - er to the max.

mo - tor - cy - cle rid - er, a high - way fly - er.
When they try to catch me, I leave them in my tracks. } I'm an out - law, ba - by,

ME AND BABY BROTHER

Words and Music by SYLVESTER ALLEN, HAROLD R. BROWN,
MORRIS DICKERSON, LONNIE JORDAN,
CHARLES W. MILLER, LEE OSKAR and HOWARD SCOTT

Moderately slow, but with a double-time feeling

Shot down Ba - by Broth - er

And they call it law and or - der!

D   A

G   A

Repeat and fade

E7#9

1.2.3. Come back Ba - by Broth - er.
4.5. Love my Ba - by Broth - er.
6.7. Come back Ba - by Broth - er.

PEACE SIGN

Words and Music by HAROLD R. BROWN,
HOWARD SCOTT and MILTON MYRICK

60

THEY CAN'T TAKE AWAY OUR MUSIC

Words and Music by SYLVESTER ALLEN, HAROLD R. BROWN,
MORRIS DICKERSON, LONNIE JORDAN,
CHARLES W. MILLER, LEE OSKAR, HOWARD SCOTT and JERRY GOLDSTEIN

Moderately slow, with a beat

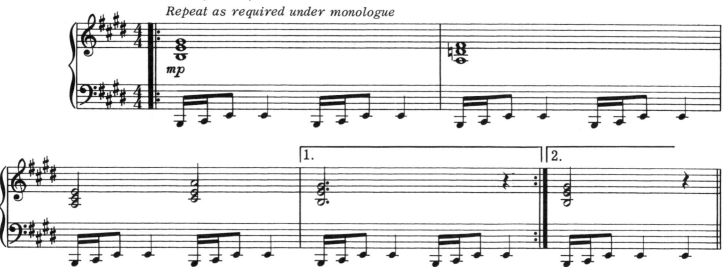

Spoken:

There's a feeling shared today,
By the people whose freedom has been taken away,
And as in the past, when times were wrong,
The common folks come together in song.
How will we win? With what will we fight?
We hope this song our world will unite.

in, it's got no hair, it's got no skin.__ As we trav-el far and

near, We bring the word for you to hear,__ And the mes-sage that we

bring, Is a - live__ in the words we sing.__ And no

mat-ter how bad you feel, We got some-thing they can't steal.__

65

Extra Lyrics

2. In the ghetto it gets cold,
But we got something to warm our souls.
Like the blanket of our faith,
Keeps us covered when we shake.
Though they take my brother's life,
And deny his given rights,
Yes the message will be heard,
As the poets spread the word.
And our spirit they can't break,
Cause we got the power to communicate, yea.

Chorus

No they can't, no they can't,
No They Can't Take Away Our Music,
No they can't, no they can't,
Say They Can't Take Away Our Music.

Fade out................

SLIPPIN' INTO DARKNESS

Words and Music by SYLVESTER ALLEN, HAROLD R. BROWN,
MORRIS DICKERSON, LONNIE JORDAN,
CHARLES W. MILLER, LEE OSKAR and HOWARD SCOTT

SPILL THE WINE

Words and Music by SYLVESTER ALLEN, HAROLD R. BROWN,
MORRIS DICKERSON, LONNIE JORDAN,
CHARLES W. MILLER, LEE OSKAR and HOWARD SCOTT

Moderate beat

Repeat as required under monologue

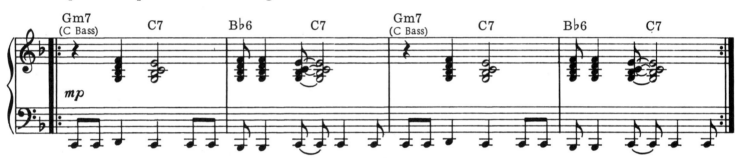

Spoken:

I was once out strolling one very hot summer's day,
When I thought I'd lay myself down to rest, in a big field of tall grass.
I lay there in the sun and felt it caressing my face.

As I fell asleep, and dreamed, I dreamed I was in a Hollywood movie,
And that I was the star of the movie.
This really blew my mind,
The fact that me, an overfed, long-haired, leaping gnome,
Should be the star of a Hollywood movie.

But there I was.
I was taken to a place, the hall of the mountain kings.
I stood high upon a mountain top, naked to the world,
In front of every kind of girl there was,
Long ones, tall ones, short ones, brown ones,
Black ones, round ones, big ones, crazy ones......

Out of the middle, came a lady.
She whispered in my ear something crazy.

She said:

Chorus

Spill The Wine and take that pearl,— Spill The Wine and take that pearl.—

Spill The Wine and take that pearl,— Spill The Wine and take that pearl.—

Extra Lyrics

Spoken:

I thought to myself what could that mean.
Am I going crazy or is this just a dream.
Now, wait a minute,
I know I'm lying in a field of grass somewhere,
So it's all in my head,
And then. . . I heard her say one more time:

Chorus:
(Sung)   Spill the wine and take that pearl,
Spill the wine and take that pearl,
Spill the wine and take that pearl,
Spill the wine and take that pearl.

Spoken:

I could feel hot flames of fire roaring at my back,
As she disappeared, but soon she returned.
In her hand was a bottle of wine, in the other, a glass.
She poured some of the wine from the bottle into the glass,
And raised it to her lips,
And just before she drank it, she said:

Chorus:
(Sung)   Spill the wine and take that pearl,
Spill the wine and take that pearl,
Spill the wine and take that pearl,
Spill the wine and take that pearl.

Fade out. . . .

SUMMER

Words and Music by SYLVESTER ALLEN, HAROLD R. BROWN,
MORRIS DICKERSON, LONNIE JORDAN,
CHARLES W. MILLER, LEE OSKAR, HOWARD SCOTT and JERRY GOLDSTEIN

WHY CAN'T WE BE FRIENDS?

Words and Music by SYLVESTER ALLEN, HAROLD R. BROWN,
MORRIS DICKERSON, LONNIE JORDAN,
CHARLES W. MILLER, LEE OSKAR, HOWARD SCOTT and JERRY GOLDSTEIN

Verse E♭   D

1. I've seen you a-round ___ for a long long time, ___
2. I see you walk-in' down in Chi - na town, ___
3. I paid my mon-ey to the wel-fare line, ___ I
4. The col - or of your skin don't mat-ter to me. ___
5. I'd kind-a like to be the pres-i - dent. ___

Cm   Cm7/F

I re - mem - bered you when you drank my ___ wine. ___
I called you but you could not turn a - round. ___
see you stand-in' in it all the time. ___
As long as I can live in har-mo - ny. ___
So I can show you how your mon-ey's ___ spent. ___

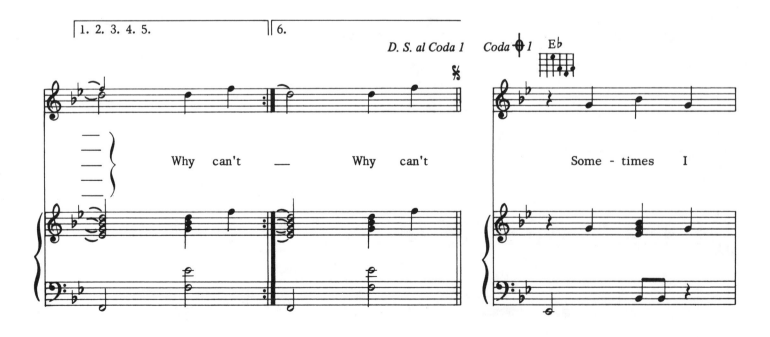

1. 2. 3. 4. 5.   6.

D. S. al Coda 1   *Coda* ⊕ *1*   E♭

Why can't ___ Why can't   Some - times I

THE WORLD IS A GHETTO

Words and Music by SYLVESTER ALLEN, HAROLD R. BROWN,
MORRIS DICKERSON, LONNIE JORDAN,
CHARLES W. MILLER, LEE OSKAR and HOWARD SCOTT

YOU GOT THE POWER

Words and Music by SYLVESTER ALLEN, HAROLD R. BROWN,
JERRY GOLDSTEIN, LONNIE JORDAN, LEE OSKAR,
HOWARD SCOTT and LUTHER RABB

WAR
ANTHOLOGY 1970 -1994
R2 71774

WAR
THE BEST OF WAR AND
MORE VOL. I
R2 70072

WAR
BEST OF WAR AND
MORE VOL.2
R2 72526

WAR
PEACE SIGN
R2 71706

WAR
WHY CAN'T WE BE
FRIENDS?
R2 71051

WAR
THE WORLD IS A
GHETTO
R2 71043

WAR
ALL DAY MUSIC
R2 71042

WAR
GALAXY
R2 71192

WAR
WAR
R2 71044

WAR
DELIVER THE WORD
R2 71259

WAR
LIVE
R2 71052

WAR
PLATINUM JAZZ
R2 71258

WAR
OUTLAW
R2 71956

WAR
LIFE (IS SO STRANGE)
R2 72288

WAR
YOUNGBLOOD
R2 72289

ERIC BURDON & WAR
ERIC BURDON
DECLARES "WAR"
R2 71050

ERIC BURDON & WAR
LOVE IS ALL AROUND
R2 71218

ERIC BURDON BAND
SUN SECRETS/STOP
R2 71219

ERIC BURDON
SINGS THE ANIMALS
GREATEST HITS
R2 71708

LEE OSKAR
LEE OSKAR
R2 71719

LEE OSKAR
MY ROAD, OUR ROAD
R2 71719

LEE OSKAR
BEFORE THE RAIN
R2 71721

LEE OSKAR
LIVE AT THE
PITT INN
R2 72628

LEE OSKAR
FREE
R2 72629